Softly Undercover

THE JOURNAL CHARLES B. WHEELER POETRY PRIZE

Softly Undercover

Hanae Jonas

MAD CREEK BOOKS, AN IMPRINT OF
THE OHIO STATE UNIVERSITY PRESS
COLUMBUS

Published by Mad Creek Books, an imprint of The Ohio State University Press.

Library of Congress Cataloging-in-Publication Data
Names: Jonas, Hanae, author.
Title: Softly undercover / Hanae Jonas.
Description: Columbus : Mad Creek Books, an imprint of The Ohio State University Press, 2024. | Series: The Journal Charles B. Wheeler poetry prize | Summary: "An elliptical, lyrical debut that explores the pleasures and hazards of ritual, devotion, divination, and illusion, examining what it means to believe"—Provided by publisher.
Identifiers: LCCN 2023040729 | ISBN 9780814258941 (paperback) | ISBN 0814258948 (paperback) | ISBN 9780814283226 (ebook) | ISBN 0814283225 (ebook)
Classification: LCC PS3610.O558 S64 2024 | DDC 811/.6—dc23/eng/20231011
LC record available at https://lccn.loc.gov/2023040729

Cover design by Susan Zucker
Text design by Juliet Williams
Type set in Adobe Garamond Pro

CONTENTS

RHODODENDRONS

Not love but procedure
I mimic
No, the stranger here will never be love
But how

to open the daily curtain
and pretend to be even
a little bit animal
alone?   Wilderness composes

itself from a rubric:
how the absent
takes cream and sugar at eight, on Sundays
wears white   Is a path

into a hell
of rhododendrons,
start that makes mad honey   Little

fix to enchant
this barren
until the real drug croons

Procedure:

how every night I gamble
on the carnality
of method   of faking it til
your ghost slides right through

THE VIEW

I lived across from a church at the back of the town. I watched

the outcomes congregate.

You are dead, you are married, you are

temporarily improved—

I annotated the strangers, imagined skipping Earth,

but people I knew around town lay wanting.

I'd posed myself: plain, quiet all summer long,

my parcel of room gone unincorporated.

Away from the pushers of nostalgia basting in memories

around every corner.

Through the glass I stared down

the church garden of statues:

their dopey expressions blank enough to serve

as canvases for other people's interests.

Any aura of solace slapped on

by prayer—vandalism disguised as love—

like spraypainted pupils, mustaches, horns, whatever

makes a body human

in the recognizable ways.

Stationed in the doorway of my safety, I understood

a statue sees in only one direction

and not very far at that.

I memorized the cost of stone, went outside.

I waited for anyone

to thrust straight through me

the length of their benevolent hands.

RITUAL FOR SPELLING SILENCE

The shade jacked open   but I'm picturing the dark

In this immaculate room   I don't even know what to say

My voice just an exercise   in how full I can get

Reenacting excess   of straight love and trouble

The old hours spent driving   towards my curly-haired doom

With dark lines   in his architecture I slept

How distant then I itched   for the boreal coming down with sun

But all those dingy rooms   precious now he's dead

I had the idea   that the sphinx rode with me

I hounded after the brume   which rose like mushrooms between rocks

I'm hounding it now   this incantation

for what was   Old flicker   I'm cupping the candle out

so this silence can become   the clank of a plowtruck

as the shade hikes high   and people in wet boots scrape into church

Do I really need angels   when the world's already bright?

How to lose the letters   the ones that sound out ghosts?

I'm coming down with morning   but still I lie flat

so I say this is a room   where no one's ever died

BLUFF LINE

To say something good
would be to ask you to stay.

Instead, I spend the days dismantling
my visibility. Once,

I showed my hand
and saw cruelty falling off,

the splinters tumbling away
for all to spectate.

I'm always at the yoke, your
constant perforations

troubling me down
to merely spine.

If you can look at me, I know
you'll swirl your fingers inside

what's left. If you look
I will concede

I'm suggestible.
Am I collapsing my life

or opening it
for good?

There's an answer you'd like
to lie down in.

Imagine good, imagine
stepping into the halo

of the sun.
To thaw

what dizzy terms we could
believe with—

APPARENT THRESHOLD

I stayed. I was a constant
hostage to mystery;

the crisis of his sights on me
was the invention of my isolation.

"He" was a series, private train
that wouldn't stop:

from its window, I watched
the sun flush

red: emergency exit

I was fenced from,
a museum.

In the diurnal distance, it fell
umber, under again:

fire in the subterranean, exhaust blowing

around the morass.
Around,

around, I couldn't

help myself through
my vote

for subjection, its impolite
fingers latching on.

Mystery,
what do you even mean about this
filmy view?

Which shut me, ill with abandon,

in a body inept
at the earthly alone.

I was a lifer. I lived away

from the defensible
empty plain, in the all-day

pool of midnight feelings

I pined
for all this beauty to end.

LOWLANDS

When I was not in love

mountains
disappeared from view

I walked
up the one hill in town
so I could pray myself down it

to begin
like a run-dead motor
skipping into gear

I walked
with one ditty looping

to swallow the perfect grid
of Sundays

swallow
the spectacle flatlining
like a Midwest street

Now this not-love
signals place

in the absence
of a rolling place

in the absence of blue yonder

Bodies
that are retrograde

don't move backwards
but appear to

It's called an apparent path

how moon arcing
invisible mountains

is not an image that exists
just words that make a line—

In love the line gestured
in arrhythmia

In love
two lines converged
and cornered me in

This is just geometry
This is just

the approach
of a limit
In love

I was immobile high on peaks

how they seemed
to pull even dirt

up to their level

AS ABOVE

To buy some

        calculation in myself,

I christened

        the brunt of him

   growth—

Immune, a weed

        open to hardening,

      the sway of drenching

or drought,

       I could take

   anything,

       wrap it tightly

like a gift: Surprise:

the blocky sky glued

       above me for years,

its lamp impalpable

        but crowding my crown.

I knew I needed   a heaven

to take me in: strange

     pet, old soul,

the kindest misnomers.

I searched for rogues

       and called them seers,

always wanting

     to see what he saw.

  Him,

him, private hymns

I made to slather heaven

        on the angry earth.

AUBADE

Like water searching for any possible wound

in the domestic weave,

the quiet days flooded with the absence of privacy

first from others, then from each other.

Nights on alert I busied myself

with the spelling of distant affections:

glut of water, supine

assembly of lies;

I tended my nocturnal devices

in which without body his tenor cut low within

my mind's vacant clip hushing

shady images,

rutted roads that led me away

until dawn. The theory

of wind in my hair, penetralia I constructed around me, my

desire in the anaretic degree.

First sight: what is possible: recoil,

its suggestive ends,

or the terse flash of the end surrounding me before

licit want can ascend.

Now that I sense the turn, I can't wait

outside myself.

The sun enters my vision;

I'm hazarding the material world.

I worry my delusion

around the fenced backyard: a brute's

guarded gnawing,

ungovernable,

to destroy an oneiric bone.

DENIALS

I stop taking notes on the minutiae
of my feelings   A few words stay near me
but no one likes them much:
magic, ritual, the mass murder
of hidden ancestors
I'm used to holding close suspect beliefs
The jury milks a law
I cannot hear now   How *bad man* (you)
was the verdict they gave
If only right now you'd roll up
to my door   our big soft talk
would shoot arrows out the window   pull
the stones right out of my chest
The deliberation of your paws
I try to conjure when I wake
startled by my body   that I haven't also
disappeared   The stranger by the fish case
says people like me
need to be careful   to not forget
I have a face
they describe like a carpet: *waiting*
to go back to where the trees work right
Xylem phloem   the patient up and down
We rolled around the loam
on generations of dead leaves   Love
didn't pool in the bathwater   No   Love
you didn't bleed right down the drain

THEN THE NIGHT IN ME WOKE UP

There isn't a way
to skim over it except

to imagine him dead. The lamp
off and I'm rifling
for courage

in the occult—for the unambiguous
smell of a tragedy
beyond my control,

to neglect that I broke
the picture glass
and shut his picture

in a book. That I couldn't
be watched because
he's defunct

by my own
damn hand: its stain across

the glossy finish
of his still, his sun-lit face.
No restoration

for such sweet cargo:
the peace he kept on a high-up hook.

Now the new metronome
raps time
into my fluted bones:

when first I saw you
I imagined silks

coming from
your pornographic mouth.

LUMINOUS CRISIS

Can't star in the play
because the plot has upset me.

Can't light your little mirror
when my blood shows on your face.

No more trying; this
time travel   insane—

Kicked open the door
and there it was
skulking—

Your wish: a marquee.
My wish:

unremarkable. One
gapless morning

at the nadir,
a warm lake.

But to shine beams on
what hangs around

the edge: an aura   of stones
a cartoon ray   of thorns.

Can't be new
but I've learned

to go softly undercover

bad faith
suspended from darkness
to darkness to—

HOMING

I have my wrong condition.

Waiting for roadkill
to wake back up. Alive

for a crayon landscape
that petitions me at night:

scribble of a hill, a little hit
of God

—to go anywhere more docile
than facts.

To wake is to wait for

admonishments on instinct. Watching

a homing animal flatten
into generic bones.

Without flesh, I can't
feel location—

I cross out names for people   this town.

Outside, the year wastes away—
Stupid sacrifice.

The calendar is making me harsh.

Day now I listen   for birds tuned to the pitch
of a haunt

from which I can't
be delivered.

GOOD

Repression's good for some things:

the long closed-door days, possession
turning my knives.

—If you can't be present
in this dollhouse   well then
I'll wish we'd never met—

Does virtue mean taking

a talent for saga, leaking it
away from sight?

I know nothing dries up and zeroes;

I touch this dead-end dampness
each damn day.

I've understood
my flawed character for a long time: womanhood

sealed and steely like a locker;
I am not about community.

When it opens, I hear the dinner plates
still shattering
around my head.

Shut it to save from running out of me:

RITUAL IN THE AFTERMATH

Everywhere the tinge of bottles, even after stasis. The bath

a glassy hull for hours starred with pins

of hair. Little floes

around the body; never will I be clean.

Around the body's imaginary life, winter-bright

belief. Now I live

inside endangered language that agrees

there's a different place.

Pretend I drag myself

down the block, past the blinking HOTEL corner, through the patrol

of frosted windows,

the hygienic minor town.

Then the gate, the stewartia stark in its garden, bark

the cast of bruises slicked

down with rime.

And the soundtrack, nondiegetic, but swelling around the body,

this bath of desperate theater for a second

trembling tall.

Day and I glaze,

day again

and his rage flaps in me, in the water

weak color between the digits where the sun never got in,

where the dead meet

the daily,

the noon slant

cool as jars.

DEAD LEXICON

You deep snow I miss   You
knee-high slosh
You shuddered down with the silence
of a subtitle the mesmerism

of moon   A little blood in the powder
You quick-spilling stain
You lacquered my neighborhood
made all words white   Showed me why

we diagram angels carve imprints
to hide inside   Take something public
make it private
again   How dearth showered down

into a child's cup   I carried it
around full of you turned into water
Tipped it back to shield
into me the last trace   How grief

froze you good in your neat white jeans
as the lights came up in the sawed-down
trees   How many kinds
of pine can I name   How many words

for rime   for wreath

CURSORY DETAILS

The bar fairly quiet, circling
around *sexual.* We sip

just water for hours
to keep the racehorse

at bay. The horse goes to sleep
but the man drives me home

anyway, asks
can we try it the next week.

The marauders in my throat
and their love

of acquiescence. I sit
on my steps like a child

who hasn't yet learned
to make her misery

an ornament; a centerfold
of the month to ripple

gaudy as swans.
What details would add

to your pleasure?
I'm just sick

in the hush
out here, not even

furniture
to keep me company.

WHAT BEAUTY

Scared—even then—
to state the obvious:

             not very white, excessive

        vocabulary for a child,
        memory

of embarrassing
precision. Answer to #1,

             privately B. The obvious mistake
             was always
                  having answers.

In the icebreaker, naming
any dumb thing that's good—

             the woolly recognition, the clairvoyant's
             line *you know*
                the trees preserve you

—saying *trees* and not *pudding*
on the first day of school,

             the metallic laughter
             of instruction entered me—

Abort spectacle,

keep the tongue
from psychic spill.

But if cleanly arranged. But half
gaijin / half new age—

Now how should I choose between discrepancies?

e.g., I carried love's knife
for practical applications

or desire is a vision
mildly coerced.

If I make a clearing
in my story, I burn

the forest down,

grow long
every hair on my body, pray

to offend what beauty
floats by.

If I pray to be seen

I become nothing.

WITH STONES AS THEIR WITNESS

There was no sawdust littering the yard
nobody wearing anybody's grandmother's ring
no one creaking the bed
getting up for a hazy piss

One time a table faced in papers
a saxophone wooing next door   Once
an overshot bedspread the jack pines
gently corroborating the deed

Which the details didn't track
but only arranged   Which was not illicit
just wholly unmappable

They were doing their time but never getting to the end

One held the other through a novel of tombs
One's imagination loomed nimbus-large
while the other kept his low to the ground, a shrub
flowering one week a year

Who fit who into the record?

The script only unfolded around
the most unremarkable cairns   Which held
no light when the public looked
into their hard blank eyes

PRIVATE PARTY

Summer swooning like a schoolboy.
I try not to picture your hands:

damp wind poring over
thin corollas,
then the dirt dirtied with pink. All day

I brood around the impasse: your
thumb's trace on my lips.

Intuit: to understand
or work out by instinct,
the method by which wind figures. Your fingers,

what are they doing
in this private party?

Their slack shape close, drippy
collar around my thoughts. Unbearable

is the air inside
summer's cathedral of moods.

EVERYTHING THAT ACTS IS ACTUAL

I shut the tired book but open
the longing song   Good to live

down here for another spell:
in the morning slums of love

the sun-crazed roads
travel into me   And his sounds dirty as lakes

Where the map grid ends
so much water begins: like a song

we listen even
to the sleeping rocks dream   the kind

of noise you can't talk about
in a book

When a road walks you this far
don't try to say

it wasn't actual:
I hear the proof

when he wakes like warm
gravel against my ear

Susurrus   sub rosa
I don't know how to keep this down

or away
from the cartographers

so I won't get sized
to faithful scale

VERSION WITH SUDDEN END

this concludes the story
of my down-low dream

        your purr a cavern
        like heavy metal

        I knelt deep

I repeated the story
framed it

as my parade

        the story goes simply

        I looked for an unfelled forest
        I applied a tourniquet

        to slow the facts

I let evening tow a veil
across your open face

        the dark
        held me good

        a seed quiescent in the ground

anything can happen
when you're still a little dead

any version perfect

in the early candles
of an unruined day

before I failed to narrate
before the dark dripped out

your face not true but near

AGAINST RITUAL

My devotion, a bad joke

pulled taut around. It's true

I loved the distance of stars

over what was obvious

down here. Flush

with the feeling of words

and no mouth to shape anything.

But who cared about that—

Not the heat with its brazen

hissing at night.

Its crescendo swelled

towards something important

but did I pick out the paramount thing?

I wanted to know

how to do fate right,

wanted to be her

numinous dog.

Maybe it's all a guess

said the night itself,

shrinking back into nothing.

I felt myself accept

this version

which would stand the test

of syrup, of innocence.

And it's true I was laughing

but couldn't stop insisting

on the starlit murmurs,

good grief,

good god.

VENUS RETROGRADE

        I carried a book
of his visions and pictured
each one. Each one

turned into trouble.
I became stoned on this trouble and then
on my proper troubles.

I wanted to feel my own weight
so each trouble enacted

this weight. I curled around
divination, its silky fur—

He was not tender   but this seemed correct.
The draft was unmoving   but it reeked: *spiritual.*
Dear danger, despite all warnings—

Sometimes you heave a cloud inside
you can't control. Sometimes

the squirming dead of summer,
it's just—

LUPINES

In those days I'd put lupines

in a jar on the table. There were women

who feared me for being a kid.

Listen, he'd say, now you call the shots

but get the pokers out of your eyes.

It was a really big time

dreaming slick by the river. I learned

to hold still so the small fish

gathered round. Imagined

getting rich would be something like that.

Blue flowers in a jar with the label still on.

A minor act of allowing

nature to come near.

How its authority

revealed me, electric and small,

my brain full of shame

and blonde hair. I was darker

than them, wrenching weeds from the yard.

But how still I could hold, how he held me

so still. Listen,

he'd say, you can always pick again.

But the jars I kept filling

with the feral blue stalks. The planets

coming round like a stray dog you fed

once. How their teeth gleamed

with a sureness, like graves.

How I came up out of it, a stone wall crumbling down.

KÜNSTLERROMAN

When I say I was a kid, I mean
I didn't know
that then I was not *adult*—

Maybe: a gripping book
in which you watched yourself steer;

a candle to illuminate the error
of the book.

This is history, you instructed
from within me,
then came. *Think*

of the dead people
who talked in this room.

Their counsel drifted
inaudibly around. In the air
had to be a blessing.

—

I felt I deserved delusion
in the service
of something large.

When you said *dead*
I knew you meant *important.*

—

I still think of you
you say from the safety
of marriage. Then, *you've changed*—

I broke a charm around my neck
that granted your fix.

It wasn't truth I liked
but its feeling.

—

I am in a room now bright
with adults just
wild

about the dead
and their theories: *the first rule*

of autobiography is that it must
be in prose—

> *What's more, this text*
> *is just a fairy tale—*

> *It couldn't have happened*
> *like that. Why does she have*
> *to rely*
> *so much on magic?*

—

Nobody sees as we do,
Patti. The bloated mantra of one
artist to another.

I learned a big word
and now I'm dull inside.

I want this book to be over.

BODY OF EVIDENCE

The flesh that remained untouched. A primal rustling

reported in the distance but no one approaching care's perimeter.

Yet night's fluky twist into a corona of rumors they made me wear. They,

the proverbial jury (out), the little neighborhood

hanging a cloud. Upon the glass spangling the snow from the back door

down to the yard. Obvious injury

to the premise but no bruise. Like I told you, no touch at all—

Whereas the mattress stolen mid-use, thrown

against the bedroom wall. His scent

of hot yeast all day long, my head cut loose to the sky.

How I too could explain

the mammal urge

to move things to the ground. Not violence

exactly: a drastic way of being on the earth: his curse.

Whereas I sailed the nightmare room on a mattress dosed with panic.

No witness around for the rapid unquilting, least of all the lying self.

Whose bony recall of gliding through the air: striking it out.

STINGING NETTLE

—Thing to get
down to:
       a rich interior life.

I understand this
is funny—already

I've gotten intimate
about my wreck. Everyone's

heard something
from me
       about sex, but

what about his body, prone,
fermenting
       on the bathroom floor?

Wouldn't sleep in our bed
out of guilt—maybe

a need to be alone
with suffering. I

lay singly but didn't
talk about it. That ritual which has
       no place.

What was inside me
was not yet

barrenness but your basic
kitchen garden—ample

but weedy, weeds ripe
for the wrenching out—
            a tract of fertile metaphor.

—Stinging nettle, bristly
            oxtongue, panic grass /
witch's hair—

How should I fill my days
now that I'm admitting
            I've got nothing?

Look into the world,
the world suggests. *Forget*

the obvious comparisons
between plants and
            your feelings.

The lavender
clouds spill over a real place
            called Michigan—

But who cares
what you call the outside

if the inside is shorn clear—
absent
            now even

of absence,
that lush
            lacerating field—

THE GLOW

Three times removed
from any grip on home.

Which place is the real life, which
has become God?

In this small town,
I'm sick
               of visitors, meaning myself;

now change is my animal
to wrangle.

               Obedient
memory: sylvan evenings,
          lossy purple sinking over

          our old yard. I heard
my whole life waiting for me—its subject,
              clear—

In practice, no one waits:
one more
          muted exit upon my return.

I'm in the minor light

of bugs afloat in a field behind the house
where history's another
          sloppy room

to pay for.

DUSK

I recurred to where relics wouldn't yield; dusk
opened in me like a dog-eared tome.

My name bore down, as if cut into
a stone
                    to preserve

any subject that shrank
from its post.

The place we slept together, quietly

bricked in, the dues
of winter stalled at the door.

Where even objects scattered feeling, like a knell—

I stilled them; still they parroted
my name made of stone.

(1) Pine bed, (2) dark window, (3) tin trinket we fingered for luck:

> a heart-shaped skull
> hovering on crude wings,

familiar to visitors of centurial graves. Death's head,
the first image permitted in the colonies—

The bridled years fraying right down the seam—

Why didn't you stay—
              a small find of grief

though typically he spoke by force of bliss. Simpler

to lose,
to lock into nothing. How to go back

if even self, an emblem?

When the Puritans came to New England
they left graves unadorned.

A loathing of icons, historians say.

But the sense is that the soul has flown away—

Here lies nowhere   snowed-over echo   the enduring
source of night.

RITUAL FOR A BACK ROOM

At the end of it I know
I was just practicing
for a dream. At times

the room winked and the dream
seemed sound. Always the same
dirty room though so blank

when dreaming.
The supernatural became
an everyday friend:

in the commute, the shower,
while suffering for someone else:
always the dream I practiced

when alone. Sometimes alone
while you were in me in the room.
The dream was not sex;

it was the completion of sex.
It was the cheekbone on the trunk
in the hallucinated room.

The possibilities felt astral
but, really, were only small.
After a time there was just

one way things could go: down
and in. I ignored this; I practiced.
And when the center spent itself flat

I woke. I don't know
what prize came, still,
from all those glinting dry runs.

IMAGINING A FOREST BY THE SEA

I can't get out of the house

when the town is like this:

symmetrical shrubs carelessly rolling

propriety around.

To love my near future is to trust

bright vernacular,

but trust sounds braver coming from any mouth

but mine. Daily

guided imagery: switching

suicide for mundanity:

now the border of what is possible

sleeps further from me yet—

Flat out in the margins. A three-card spread ending

with Oppression.

Have I reached the periphery of my survival

on romantic sweep?

The lush undergrowth of his care

proportional to the exit of urgent images

which once I spilled freely,

excess trash around town.

I am not special, not even

very psychic.

Just shutting my eyes

for long periods of time.

DELINQUENTS

I placed myself outside of mystery.

Then before you I was a stone

stopped at a steep edge, hard
in my feverish control.

Did I miss you immediately
or never,

you who I felt immediately
I should look away from?

In an unmysterious world, the answer
would always be never.

Never: a world without symbols
or indecent intuition, this

nothing, this public space.

Trust nothing—

You said clarity is an illusion.
I said illusion's an accessory

to crime. Suddenly

I was peering into a familiar
abandoned room,

an alarming privacy waiting inside.

I wanted
to surrender speech: I wanted you
to pull the words out from in me.

If ever I called myself safe, I was a liar.

I, who believed myself finally
impermeable to omens,
the tired jailer of so much trouble,

the old symbols piled up
around me
like bills—

I left them but they didn't leave me.

No, the world will not leave me be.

IT SAYS NOTHING

I try to draw your face, how it clears

my crosses as I sleep.

How it says nothing, but sanguine futures stream out.

A document I could give you

that's not this story in puddled grays; this is a study

not of you but of my nail-biting.

The lucid minutes I draw, then stray

to the ephemeris,

hunt validation of the established arrangement, kick around

the cramped sights, other brows I loved—

which are historical, thus describable, thus

out, tedious drafts.

But the black spot of your eye adream, now the talk

of my worn pillow,

yet interpretable merely

as warped circles on the page.

If I can't even draw you, how can you believe

in confession, this explicit lack?   How can

the violets and blues float with you,

free of sentence   free

of spell

IMAGINING A FOREST BY THE SEA

Self-slaking exile into the land of weeping spruces.

I still know in the right landscape
how to stay.

How to remain close
to the earth
or any range they'd call alive—

If not my ugly evidence, I am

still armed by illusion
of sororal touch:

lank grasses under
my hands.

Safe from the guidebook: my extant capacity

to defect
to the flushed logic of deceit—

Scandal inside of which

no contract with the drab.

No drowsy silt   always up ahead.

No use
for dark doorways

to leave through.

ACKNOWLEDGMENTS

Thank you to the editors of *Bennington Review, BOAAT, Columbia: A Journal of Literature and Art, Denver Quarterly, DREGINALD, Dusie, Four Way Review, H_NGM_N, Handsome*, the *Iowa Review, The Journal, jubilat, NECK, Powder Keg Magazine, Twelfth House, The Volta, West Branch,* and *ZYZZYVA* for publishing earlier versions of these poems. Several poems also appeared in a chapbook, *Lowlands,* published by Albion Books—thank you to Brian Teare.

Thank you to Marcus Jackson, The Ohio State University Press, and *The Journal* for bringing this book into the world. Thank you to Rose Marasco for allowing me to reproduce *Circle No. 1* on the cover.

For gifts of time, space, community, and money that enabled this work, thank you to the University of Michigan, the Vermont Studio Center, the Virginia Center for the Creative Arts, Kundiman, Ox-Bow School of Art, Mineral School, and the Stadler Center for Poetry & Literary Arts.

Thank you to my teachers, especially Linda Gregerson, Tung-Hui Hu, Laura Kasischke, Tarfia Faizullah, Joan Larkin, Ellen Doré Watson, and G. C. Waldrep. Thank you to my poetry cohort at the University of Michigan, whose feedback and comradery shaped the earliest version of this book. For crucial friendship/readership, special thanks to Emily Chew, Clare Needham, and Hannah Webster.

Thanks to my family.

Finally, for reading and talking about these poems, and for living through them with me, thank you to Sean St. Charles.

NOTES

"Lowlands" is written after Saskia Hamilton's poem "Slow Train."

The title "Then the Night in Me Woke Up" is adapted from a line in Fanny Howe's poem "A Hymn."

The title "With Stones as Their Witness" is inspired by "With Grass as Their Witness" by C. D. Wright.

"Everything That Acts Is Actual" borrows its title from Denise Levertov. The italicized lines are adapted from Jonathan Edwards via Susan Howe's *My Emily Dickinson*.

The claim in "Künstlerroman" that autobiography must be in prose comes from Philippe Lejeune's essay "The Autobiographical Pact." The final section of the poem quotes *Just Kids* by Patti Smith.

In "Dusk," the line "But the sense is that the soul has flown away" is borrowed from the article "The Evolution of the Death's Head" by Loren Rhoads, published on cemeterytravel.com.

"Imagining a Forest by the Sea" references the Ten of Wands, also known in the Thoth tarot as the Lord of Oppression. The card signifies restriction and thwarted will.

In "Delinquents," the lines "Did I miss you immediately / or never" are inspired by lines from Marni Ludwig's poem "Expert on Shadows."

THE JOURNAL CHARLES B. WHEELER POETRY PRIZE